DOES THE BIBLE REALLY SAY I AM GOOD ENOUGH FOR HEAVEN?

(FIND OUT THE SURPRISING REAL GOOD NEWS!)

DR. JOHN M. STROHMAN

Published by:
Cross Centered Press
113 Village Drive
Pierre, SD 57501

Copyright 2019, 2020, John Strohman. Copies of various sections can be made as long as they are used for the furtherance of the Gospel of Jesus Christ and are freely given away. Otherwise, all rights reserved and no part of this publication may be reproduced, transmitted, recorded or distributed without prior written permission of Cross Centered Press or the author.

Softcover ISBN: 978-1-7343262-0-8
Hardcover ISBN: 978-1-7343262-2-2
Kindle - Mobi (e-book) ISBN: 978-1-7343262-3-9
E-Pub (e-book) ISBN: 978-1-7343262-4-6

Unless otherwise noted, verses are cited from the *New American Standard Bible* 1977 edition and 1995 update. *The New American Standard Bible®*, Copyright 1960, 1962, 1963, 1968, 1971, 1972, 1973, 1975, 1977, 1995 by the The Lockman Foundation.

Some references or portions in this book originate from other works of this author including: *The Application Commentary of the Gospel of Matthew;* Softcover ISBN: 978-0-9859949-0-7, Hardcover ISBN: 978-0-9859949-7-6, Kindle (eBook) ISBN: 978-0-9859949-1-4, E-Pub (eBook) ISBN 978-0-9859949-2-1 and *The Fake Commission:* Softcover ISBN: 978-0-9859949-3-8, Hardcover ISBN: 978-0-9859949-6-9, Kindle (eBook) ISBN: 978-0-9859949-4-5, E-Pub (eBook) ISBN: 978-0-9859949-5-2.

Edition 9-20

ABOUT THE AUTHOR

The most distinguishing feature of the author is that he is

a sinner who, in his early youth, was saved from the judgment to come by the grace of God. He continues to recognize his complete reliance on the mercy, forgiveness and grace of Jesus Christ <u>to this very moment</u>.

* Other matters:

John M. Strohman is a graduate of the University of Iowa College of Business and earned his Juris Doctor from the University of South Dakota School of Law. He has served as an Assistant Attorney General for the State of South Dakota. As an attorney with over thirty years of experience, he has handled a variety of cases in state and federal court, including serving as counsel for more than 200 cases before the South Dakota Supreme Court. John has also held faculty positions as an adjunct professor for South Dakota State University, Liberty University, Northern State University and Colorado Christian University. His teaching experience has spanned both the undergraduate and graduate level. In 2012 he authored *The Application Commentary of the Gospel of Matthew (2019 Final Edition)*. In 2014 he authored *The Fake Commission (2017 update)*. He has served on mission boards and is the current chairman of Cross Centered Missions. John and his wife, Sarah, share a passion for equipping young people in Christian service through discipleship, Sunday school, Bible studies and leading short-term mission trips.

[The author does not receive any personal royalties from the sales of this book. All royalties go directly to further world missions. The opinions contained herein are the author's and do not represent any other person, institution or organization.]

INTRODUCTION

Please take a few minutes and read this entire book. Seriously, take my advice and do not skim or page through it, but take the time to read it. It is so important you truly understand the issue and realize the eternal consequences it has for you.

TABLE OF CONTENTS

(Chapter 1)
AFTER WHAT?
Page 5

(Chapter 2)
NOW YOU ANSWER THE QUESTIONS!
Page 11

(Chapter 3)
GOD WILL AUTOMATICALLY FORGIVE ME ...right?
Page 19

(Chapter 4)
DOES THE BIBLE REALLY SAY I AM GOOD ENOUGH FOR HEAVEN?
Page 23

(Chapter 5)
THE REAL GOOD NEWS.
Page 27

(Appendix 1)
UNITED STATES v. GEORGE WILSON
UNITED STATES SUPREME COURT CASE
Page 31

(Appendix 2)
A GENERAL OUTLINE OF FOUNDATIONAL DOCTRINES OF BIBLICAL CHRISTIANITY.
Page 36

CHAPTER 1

AFTER WHAT?

Below are a few snapshots of different stages of life. At each stage, the individual has engaged in some preparation in hopes of success.

- A teenager dedicates several hundred hours and thousands of dollars in training and preparation with the hope of securing a varsity position on a high school sports team.

- A college student dedicates many years and tens-of-thousands of dollars in education and preparation with the hope of securing a good job.

- A seventy-year-old dedicates five decades of work and hundreds of thousands of dollars in savings and preparation with the hope of securing a comfortable retirement…before his death.

What is the reality in each situation? The teenager may only make the varsity team for a couple of years. The college student may only find good employment for fifty years. The wealthy

Ch. 1: AFTER WHAT?

retiree may only be healthy and active for another ten years.

I would ask each person, "What about after that?" To which each would most likely respond: "After what?" I would explain my question by saying: "After your sport is done, your work is over, or your retired body expires, what then?"

Most people are stumped by the question. We all strongly agree it is wise to plan, work and save throughout our lives, so that we can be as comfortable as possible...on our way to the grave. Yet, it is amazing how little thought is given to what happens next.

People are so focused on trying to live for eighty years, they give only passing thoughts to the eternity following them. Jesus said in John 6:27:

> *"Do not work for the food which perishes, but for the food which endures to eternal life, which the Son of Man will give to you..."*

Worse yet, there are people who do not want to even think about what happens after life ends. Burying your head in the sand is not a good plan to resolve any issue, let alone one of eternal significance.

I find that everyone has some opinion regarding what happens to a person when one dies. What is yours? Where did you form your opinion? Why do you think your opinion is true? Are you willing to bet all that you have on it, including your own soul? Most people will admit their view is a mixture of personal philosophy and some opinions they have heard over time. Ultimately, most desire a view of death that either results in them feeling good about themselves or feeling nothing at all. Yet, everyone will admit having moments in which they have considered their own mortality (and that is why life insurance companies have such big buildings). The statistic remains the same, 10 out of 10 people will die at some time.

Think of the funerals you have attended. I am sure most included a religious leader who went to great lengths to comfort the family. Often this is expressed by assuring them that the dead person has "gone on to a better place." If you read the deceased person's obituary, you can understand that opinion. In about four or five paragraphs it states that the person was friendly, worked hard, took care of his/her family, and belonged to some civil, charitable, or religious organization.

On the other hand, you may have attended the funeral of someone who was not so good. Worse yet, the person may have been bad, like a convicted felon (or even a murderer)! The

Ch. 1: AFTER WHAT?

confusing part is that the same religious leader will likewise go to great lengths to assure the family that despite the deceased's "struggles in life," at least he/she has "gone on to a better place." In addition, it will be inferred (if not stated) that the person is "now in the comfort and presence of God."

Can both scenarios be true? If so, how can the religious leader step back into that same pulpit Sunday morning and talk about Hell? So, when is he telling the truth? Is he lying to the deceased person's family, or lying to the congregation about Heaven and Hell? What is the truth about what happens to you after you die? DOES THE BIBLE REALLY SAY I AM GOOD ENOUGH FOR HEAVEN?

I have been an attorney for more than thirty years. Throughout those years, I have spent time with a wide variety of people. Some of them could be categorized as either very good or very bad. For example, I have been around some very upstanding and generous people. On the other hand, I have also prosecuted those who have stolen, raped, and even killed. I mention my training as an attorney because it impacts how I will answer the question, "DOES THE BIBLE REALLY SAY I AM GOOD ENOUGH FOR HEAVEN?" As an attorney, I am a person of evidence. Thus, I do not approach the question with the slightest concern for church affiliation, denominations, religious leaders, traditions, cults, metaphysics or organizations' claims. I don't even care what my family, friends, skeptics, scientists, and atheists may speculate happens once a person dies. The question is an all-important question; I want to be sure; I want to only know the TRUTH! Especially when I am banking *my own* eternity on it. Jesus Himself said, "…the truth shall make you free." John 8:32.

This is a very short book and I encourage you to take a few minutes and read it to completion. There will be a few surprises along the way, but by the end, like it or not, you will know the truth…assuming you do not skim or quit along the way. Just so you know, I have zero interest in you joining some organization, voting a certain way, giving money to an institution or doing some religious exercise. My intent is that you know the true answer to the question, "DOES THE BIBLE REALLY SAY I AM GOOD ENOUGH FOR HEAVEN?" What you do with that truth is your responsibility.

This book is not intended to be an academic defense of the Bible, but I will say that I have studied the Bible for more than forty years. Why the Bible? Because I have experienced what the Bible states in Psalm 12:6:

"The words of the Lord are pure words;
As silver tried in a furnace on the earth,
refined seven times."

Ch. 1: AFTER WHAT?

The Bible states in 2 Timothy 3:16-17:
> *"All Scripture is inspired by God and profitable for teaching, for reproof, for correction, for training in righteousness; that the man of God may be adequate, equipped for every good work."*

The Bible is constantly misrepresented by all kinds of people (including religious leaders) who frankly do not know what it says or deliberately distort it. It seems everyone is a street theologian. Everyone has an opinion about God and the Bible whether they actually know anything or not. I have run into many who say they do not believe the Bible. When I ask if they have read it, they quickly claim that they have. When I test their claim, via a few Bible-knowledge questions, they will admit they have read "parts" of the Bible. Very few can honestly state they have read the entire New Testament from Matthew to Revelation, let alone the entire Bible.

CHAPTER 2

NOW YOU ANSWER THE QUESTIONS!

After multiple examinations of the entire text of the Old and New Testament (in context) I am more sure of its complete reliability and authority than I am of anything in life. With that being said, the Bible, viewed in context, has clear conclusions that can be drawn and may surprise you. True Christianity -

- Is not about earning your way to Heaven by being kind and helping the poor.

- Is not about earning your way to Heaven by living a clean, moral life, or getting rid of some sins and doing more good things than bad.

- Is not about earning your way to Heaven by going to church each week and reciting the Apostles' Creed or saying the Lord's Prayer multiple times.

- Is not about earning your way to Heaven by engaging in a religious ritual such as: baptism, communion, penance, confession, or saying a prayer.

Ch. 2: NOW YOU ANSWER THE QUESTIONS!

Here is what the Bible says about humans: Psalm 53:1–3:
> The fool has said in his heart, "There is no God," They are corrupt, and have committed abominable injustice; There is no one who does good. God has looked down from heaven upon the sons of men to see if there is anyone who understands, who seeks after God. Every one of them has turned aside; together they have become corrupt; there is no one who does good, not even one.

Maybe you are not willing to accept this truth. You feel comfortable lifting up your head and saying, "I may not be perfect, but I am a good person." There is your fatal error: God's standard is not "good"...it is *PERFECTION*. God does not grade on a curve. We may tolerate a certain amount of lying and cheating from others, because we too lie and cheat. With God, there are only two categories of people: You are either in the "perfect" group or "not perfect" group. Jesus Himself said in Matthew 5:48, *"Therefore you are to be perfect, as your heavenly Father is perfect."* I would strongly encourage you to take the five-question, "Good Person Final Exam" to see if you are good enough to get into Heaven.

GOOD PERSON FINAL EXAM

To start this Final Exam, we will turn to God's standard of righteousness, His Royal Law – THE TEN COMMANDMENTS, found in Exodus 20:3-17. Have you obeyed God's law perfectly…in every thought…in every word…and in every deed…for every second of your life, like Jesus Christ? Let's start by writing down your answers to the following questions:

- One of the commandments is: *"You shall not bear false witness…."* Exodus 20:16.

    QUESTION 1: Have you ever, in your entire life, told a single lie? How many lies have you told?

    > We would all agree that a person who does not tell the truth is called a liar. Are you *perfect* or are you a liar? Revelation 21:8 says *"… and all liars, their part will be in the lake that burns with fire and brimstone, which is the second death."*

    YOUR ANSWER: _____
    _____

Ch. 2: NOW YOU ANSWER THE QUESTIONS!

- Another commandment is: *"You shall not steal."* Exodus 20:15.

  <u>QUESTION 2:</u> Have you ever, in your entire life, taken anything that did not belong to you? (Remember, it does not matter if it was of small value or that the theft took place a long time ago.)

  > We all agree that a person who has stolen something is called a thief. Are you *perfect* or are you a thief?

  YOUR ANSWER: _____

- Another commandment is: *"You shall not take the name of the Lord your God in vain."* Exodus 20:7.

  <u>QUESTION 3:</u> Have you ever, in your entire life, used God's name in vain through swearing or disrespectful slang like saying, "Oh, My G_d!" Have you ever said God or Jesus' name as a curse word, or to express disgust? The Bible says *"… for the Lord will not leave him unpunished who takes His name in vain."* Exodus 20:7.

> A person who uses God's name in vain is called a blasphemer. Are you *perfect* or are you a blasphemer of the holy name of God?
>
> YOUR ANSWER: _____

- Another commandment is: *"You shall not commit adultery."* Exodus 20:14. Maybe you think you have not committed the act of adultery, but Jesus stated in Matthew 5:28 that the one who looks at another with lust has *"committed adultery...already"* in his/her heart.

QUESTION 4: Have you ever in your entire life committed adultery, or at one time looked upon another with lust?

> A person who commits adultery; or looks with lust (sexual desire) at another who is not their spouse, is an adulterer at heart. Are you *perfect* or are you an adulterer; or one who has committed adultery in your heart?
>
> YOUR ANSWER: _____

Ch. 2: NOW YOU ANSWER THE QUESTIONS!

- Another commandment is: *"You shall not murder."* Exodus 20:13. Maybe you can claim to not have murdered anyone, but have you ever hated anyone? The Bible says that if you hate someone you are a murderer! 1 John 3:15: *"Everyone who hates his brother is a murderer; and you know that no murderer has eternal life abiding in him."*

  > **QUESTION 5:** Have you ever, in your entire life, either murdered someone or had a quick flash of hate for someone? Are you perfect or at best, a murderer at heart?
  >
  > YOUR ANSWER: _____

The Good Person Final Exam covered only five of God's Ten Commandments (there are five more Commandments that you must also have perfectly obeyed). These include never desiring somebody else's property and always having God first in every part of your life. If you are even slightly honest you know you have broken God's law as set out in the Ten Commandments. Your criminal violations against God are not simply a few "here and there" but thousands and thousands of lawless thoughts, words and deeds against God throughout your life. Even if you only had one violation of God's law, you are not perfect, and guilty of violating all of God's law:

> James 2:10: *"For whoever keeps the whole law and yet stumbles in one point, he has become guilty of all."*
>
> 1 John 1:8: *"If we say that we have no sin, we are deceiving ourselves and the truth is not in us."*

Now that you have taken the test, do you still think you are truly a "good person" by God's standard? Remember, God's Law requires you to perfectly obey His Commandments (in thought, word and deed) your entire life. It was Jesus who said in Matthew 5:48: *"Therefore you are to be perfect, as your heavenly Father is perfect."*

So, what is the verdict for your life? If you died in the next five minutes would God judge you as innocent or guilty of violating even one of His laws set out in the Ten Commandments? If you are slightly honest, you must admit you are GUILTY! Everyone fails God's perfect standard. It does not matter how you line up in society as either good, bad or somewhere in-between, since that is not the standard. God's standard is absolute perfection. God is in the perfect category, and everyone else is in the not perfect / sinner category.

Ch. 2: NOW YOU ANSWER THE QUESTIONS!

The Bible says in the Book of Hebrews 9:27 that *"...it is appointed for men to die once and after this comes judgment...."* So, since you are an admitted serial criminal offender of God's Holy Law, do you think you would go to Heaven or Hell? If you are slightly honest, you know you are guilty as... literal Hell.[1]

---

[1] Some information above regarding a "good person test" by using the Ten Commandments comes from Ray Comfort. See R. Comfort and K. Cameron, The School of Biblical Evangelism (Bridge-Logos Publishers, 2004.)

CHAPTER 3

GOD WILL AUTOMATICALLY FORGIVE ME
...right?

Some will say God is so loving and forgiving, He will automatically pretend you did not commit the sins / crimes that you actually did. The falseness of that view is the result of not understanding that the Bible clearly sets forth that God is perfectly holy, and thus all sin must be judged. God does not marginalize His holiness or His forgiveness. God is not some gray-haired grandpa who knows you are a rascal, but with a wink and a smile, opens the doors of Heaven to let you slip in anyway. Those who hold to such a view demonstrate a complete lack of understanding regarding the severity of sin in light of a Perfect God. The Bible tells us how God views the ungodly. In Psalm 7:11 (NKJV) *"...God is angry with the wicked every day."* When is the last time you heard a religious leader read that verse during a sermon...or mention it at a funeral? The reason there is a funeral, is because there is physical death. One suffers physical death as the result of their sin. Romans 6:23 tells us that *"the wages of sin is death...."* After physical death is the judgement. Hebrews 9:27 states that *"...it is appointed for men to die once and after this comes*

Ch. 3: GOD WILL AUTOMATICALLY FORGIVE ME...RIGHT?

judgment...." And after the judgement comes the second death in Hell, (see Revelation 21:8).

It would be foolish to not seriously examine what the Bible states is the punishment for those who tell a single lie. Revelation 21:8: *"...and all liars, their part will be in the lake that burns with fire and brimstone, which is the second death."*

Are you mentioned in any of the categories listed below in 1 Corinthians 6:9–11?
"Or do you not know that the unrighteous will not inherit the kingdom of God? Do not be deceived; neither fornicators, nor idolaters, nor adulterers, nor effeminate, nor homosexuals, nor thieves, nor the covetous, nor drunkards, nor revilers, nor swindlers, will inherit the kingdom of God. Such were some of you; but you were washed, but you were sanctified, but you were justified in the name of the Lord Jesus Christ and in the Spirit of our God."

I have seen many religious leaders who were more concerned about their own financial well-being than another's eternal soul. These phony religious leaders want the money to come in and you to like them. These false teachers will gladly assure you by saying, "Jesus would never send a good person like you to Hell." Many of these charlatans will go a step further and claim there is no Hell. That may sound nice, but remember, the objective here is to tell you the truth about what Jesus said. Jesus Himself repeatedly warns us of the torment of Hell. A study of Jesus' teaching shows He taught more about Hell than He did about love. Here are some of Jesus' actual words regarding Hell.

Matthew 13:41–42:
> *"The Son of Man will send forth His angels, and they will gather out of His kingdom all stumbling blocks, and those who commit lawlessness, and <u>will throw them into the furnace of fire; in that place there will be weeping and gnashing of teeth."</u>*

Matthew 25:41:
> *"Then He will also say to those on His left, 'Depart from Me, accursed ones, into the <u>eternal fire</u> which has been prepared for the devil and his angels....'"*

Matthew 25:46:
> *"These will go away into <u>eternal punishment</u>, but the righteous into eternal life."*

Mark 9:43:
> *"If your hand causes you to stumble, cut it off; it is better for you to enter life crippled, than, having your two hands, <u>to go into hell, into the unquenchable fire</u>...."*

Ch. 3: GOD WILL AUTOMATICALLY FORGIVE ME...RIGHT?

Matthew 10:28:
> [28] *"Do not fear those who kill the body but are unable to kill the soul; but rather fear Him who is able to <u>destroy both soul and body in hell</u>."*

In summary, Jesus makes it clear that: 1) there is a Hell and, 2) people go to Hell forever.

With this as a foundation, we are now ready to answer the question that served as the title of this book.

CHAPTER 4

DOES THE BIBLE REALLY SAY I AM GOOD ENOUGH FOR HEAVEN?

The bad news is that despite your positive and delightful thoughts about your own goodness, you have lived as an enemy of God,[2] a violator of His law, and one day will be rightfully judged by Christ to punishment in the fires of Hell for all eternity.[3] So based on our own righteousness, the Bible definitely states that NONE OF US ARE GOOD ENOUGH TO GO TO HEAVEN. Not only are we unable to earn Heaven, but we will

---

[2] James 4:4: "*You adulteresses, do you not know that friendship with the world is hostility toward God? Therefore whoever wishes to be a friend of the world makes himself an enemy of God.*"

[3] Jesus said in John 7:7: "*The world cannot hate you, but it hates Me because I testify of it, that its deeds are evil.*" (Review the verses below).
  o Romans 8:7: "*...because the mind set on the flesh is hostile toward God; for it does not subject itself to the law of God, for it is not even able to do so.*"
  o 1 Peter 4:5: "*but they will give account to Him who is ready to judge the living and the dead.*"
  o Matthew 13:49–50: "*So it will be at the end of the age; the angels will come forth and take out the wicked from among the righteous, [50]and will throw them into the furnace of fire; in that place there will be weeping and gnashing of teeth.*"
  o Revelation 20:15: "*And if anyone's name was not found written in the book of life, he was thrown into the lake of fire.*"
  o Matthew 23:33: "*You serpents, you brood of vipers, how will you escape the sentence of hell?*"

rightfully be judged to Hell for our sin. The Bible also states that…IT DOES NOT HAVE TO END THIS WAY!

God is righteous. Because He is righteous, He cannot pretend you did not violate His law. God cannot ignore sin, just like a good judge cannot ignore a murderer or a child molester brought before the court for punishment. God's justice requires a person to be doomed upon one violation of His law. This God of perfect justice is also an incredibly kind and loving God. While we were still enemies of God's, His love for us provided a way to be forgiven. Romans 5:8–10 states:

"But God demonstrates His own love toward us, in that while we were yet sinners, Christ died for us. Much more then, having now been justified by His blood, we shall be saved from the wrath of God through Him. For if while we were enemies we were reconciled to God through the death of His Son, much more, having been reconciled, we shall be saved by His life."

Jesus was not subject to the death penalty for any personal sin, because He never sinned, not even once in thought, word or deed. Why was He sinless? Because He is God the Son. You see, God the Father, sent His innocent Son, Jesus, who willingly offered his life as a substitute to pay the guilty sinner's death penalty. The innocent Jesus' sacrificial death on the cross satisfied God's justice, anger and punishment against the criminal sinner. Although humanity did not deserve Jesus' great sacrifice, without it, no one would have any hope in being forgiven. Now you know why the Bible tells us that "...God is love." 1 John 4:8.

It is very important to understand that God's forgiveness does *not* automatically apply to everyone. It applies to only those who put their faith in Jesus' sacrificial death on the cross as the sole basis of their forgiveness. "It is one thing to believe in God; it is another thing to believe God. To believe God, to trust in Him for our very life, is the essence of the Christian faith."[4]

The term "gospel" means "good news." The real good news is that no matter how great is the evil you have done; you can be forgiven by God and escape eternal punishment in Hell. Not only will you escape the torture of eternal damnation, but God will grant you eternal life to dwell with Him in Heaven forever!

You may ask, "How can this happen?" God tells you to turn from your sins and put your faith only in the work of the sinless Lord Jesus Christ. The real Jesus of the Bible is God's Son, the

---

[4] Sproul, R. C., *Essential Truths of the Christian Faith*, Topic 64 – Faith (Wheaton, Illinois: Tyndale House Publishers, Inc.) 1992.

Almighty God, who died on the Cross to take the eternal punishment for your sins. He proved that He was God by rising from the dead.

The person who does not believe only in Jesus, for his/her own salvation, remains an unforgiven violator of the Law of God and an enemy of God. Look again at Romans 5:10: *"For if while we were enemies we were reconciled to God through the death of His Son, much more, having been reconciled, we shall be saved by His life."* This verse points out the power of God's love in that while we were His enemy, He provided a way for us to be saved through Jesus Christ's sacrifice on the cross. Why? Because God states in Ezekiel 33:11: *"As I live! declares the Lord GOD, I take no pleasure in the death of the wicked, but rather that the wicked turn from his way and live. Turn back, turn back from your evil ways!"* In John 3:16-18 the Bible states:

> *"For God so loved the world, that He gave His only begotten Son, that whoever believes in Him shall not perish, but have eternal life. For God did not send the Son into the world to judge the world, but that the world might be saved through Him. He who believes in Him is not judged; he who does not believe has been judged already, because he has not believed in the name of the only begotten Son of God."*

CHAPTER 5

THE REAL GOOD NEWS.

The word gospel means "good news." The gospel is not complex. God's plan is not for you to have a carefree life, full of health and wealth. God's plan is that you repent and believe the gospel, and thus escape the judgment to come. For God, "... *is patient toward you, not wishing for any to perish but for all to come to repentance."* 2 Peter 3:9. This is what the Apostles preached: Acts 20:21: *"...solemnly testifying to both Jews and Greeks of <u>repentance toward God and faith in our Lord Jesus Christ</u>."* This is what Jesus preached in Mark 1:14-15: *"... Jesus came into Galilee, preaching the gospel of God, and saying, 'The time is fulfilled, and the kingdom of God is at hand; <u>repent and believe in the gospel</u>.'"*

- To *REPENT* means to turn from your sins and forsake them by the power of God.[5]

---

[5] "The power of God" – meaning when one is born again by the Spirit of God as set out in John 3:5-6. This is not a person who is trying on his/her own to clean themself up.

Note that the concept of "believing in Jesus" is more than simply agreeing with some facts about Jesus. A person is spiritually dead and it is the act of God that allows one to see the kingdom of God: *"Truly, truly, I say to you, unless one is born again he cannot see the kingdom of God."* John chapter 3 is not an explanation on *how* to get

Ch. 5: THE <u>REAL</u> GOOD NEWS.

- **To *BELIEVE THE GOSPEL* means that one who is "born again" by the Spirit of God (John 3:3-8) will:**
  - Believe in Jesus Christ as Almighty God, who is without sin;
  - Believe in Jesus' sacrificial death on the cross as the only and complete payment for your sins;
  - Believe in Jesus' bodily resurrection from the dead on the third day; and
  - Believe in Jesus as Lord over all things and confesses this fact to others.

It is that straightforward. Salvation has nothing to do with your self-righteousness, good works, engaging in a religious ceremony, or cleaning yourself up first to try to earn God's acceptance. The Bible clearly states that on your own, you are not good enough for heaven and you can do nothing to earn it. In Ephesians 2:8–9 it states: *"For by grace you have been saved through faith; and that not of yourselves, it is the gift of*

---

born again; it is an explanation that it is a work of the Spirit of God. John 3:3–8: *"Jesus answered and said to him, 'Truly, truly, I say to you, unless one is born again he cannot see the kingdom of God.' Nicodemus said to Him, 'How can a man be born when he is old? He cannot enter a second time into his mother's womb and be born, can he?' Jesus answered, 'Truly, truly, I say to you, unless one is born of water and the Spirit he cannot enter into the kingdom of God. That which is born of the flesh is flesh, and that which is born of the Spirit is spirit. Do not be amazed that I said to you, 'You must be born again.' The wind blows where it wishes and you hear the sound of it, but do not know where it comes from and where it is going; so is everyone who is born of the Spirit.'"*

God; not as a result of works, so that no one may boast." It is all about Jesus Christ, and His love, mercy, forgiveness and glory. If you reject God's loving gift of forgiveness in Jesus Christ, you remain a guilty sinner waiting to be punished in eternal Hell (see John 3:36). In summary: despite all the evil you have done, God's Word says that you can be forgiven and granted eternal life through Jesus Christ alone. The Bible says in John 3:36: *"He who believes in the Son has eternal life; but he who does not obey the Son will not see life, but the wrath of God abides on him."* If you *truly believe*, you are saved for all eternity! The Bible says so:

> 1 John 5:13: *"These things I have written to you who believe in the name of the Son of God, in order that you may know that you have eternal life."*

You do not know the day or the hour that you will attend your own funeral. Repent and believe the gospel TODAY, before it is too late!

Now you know the truth about what happens to you after you die.

APPENDIX 1 of 2

UNITED STATES v. GEORGE WILSON
UNITED STATES SUPREME COURT
(January 1833 term)

The response to Christ's sacrifice and forgiveness is either acceptance or rejection. In Hebrews 2:3 it states, *"how shall we escape if we neglect so great a salvation?...."* Many will neglect or even reject such salvation, even though there is no escape for them. For example, say you were convicted of a Federal crime and rightfully sat on death row for that crime. According to the law, only one person has the authority to pardon you of that sentence. How would you respond if that person actually granted you a pardon? Would you just ignore it, or grab onto it, like your life depended on it (because it does)? Let's look at a real Supreme Court case that involved those issues.

In 1833 the United State Supreme Court, decided the case of United States v. George Wilson.[6] Wilson had a Federal conviction that resulted in a death sentence.[7]

---

[6] UNITED STATES v. GEORGE WILSON 32 U.S. 150, 7 Pet. 150, 8 L.Ed. 640 (UNITED STATES SUPREME COURT January 1833 term).

[7] Id. 32 U.S. at 151

Although doomed by the death sentence, he was saved when he was issued a pardon from the only person who could grant it, the President of the United States, Andrew Jackson.[8] One must realize the pardon was sent directly to Wilson himself and not to the sentencing court. The Supreme Court specifically held that a pardon is a private communication by the President to the defendant, and not to the Court.

A bizarre turn of events occurred when Wilson refused to formally make the Court aware of his pardon! Technically, the Court was aware that the pardon was floating around out there, but Wilson did not actually produce it so that the Court could stop his execution. With that factual background, you can see that the issue before the Supreme Court was <u>whether the Court could force a pardon upon someone</u>. In answering that question, the Court first explained what a pardon is:

> "<u>A pardon is an act of grace,</u> proceeding from the power entrusted with the execution of the laws, <u>which exempts the individual, on whom it is bestowed, from the punishment the law inflicts for a crime he has committed.</u>" [9]

---

[8] Wilson was granted a pardon on June 14, 1830. Id at 153.

[9] Id. at 160.

The Court went on to explain that the pardon had no effect unless it was accepted by the criminal:

> "<u>A pardon is a deed</u>, to the validity of which, delivery is essential, and <u>delivery is not complete without acceptance. It may then be rejected by the person to whom it is tendered; and if it be rejected, we have discovered no power in a court to force it on him.</u>" [10]

You are like George Wilson. You know you are guilty of violating God's law and that eternal judgment is coming soon. The only person in all creation who can pay for your sins is the perfect Son of God, Jesus Christ, who has died on the cross to pay your death penalty. He offers you a complete pardon because of His love for you. Will you, with great joy and appreciation, embrace that pardon and tell others? Or maybe you are like Wilson and say, "Yes, I may have done something wrong, but I am a tough guy, and I will take what's coming." That type of response shows you have a complete ignorance of the justice and wrath of God. Realize, you are facing judgment for all eternity in fiery Hell!

---

[10] Id at 161.

It is my prayer that you will repent (turn from your sins and forsake them) and put your faith in the Lord Jesus Christ to be the total payment for your sins. Right now, call upon Him to forgive you and save you from the judgment to come. He will receive you and forgive you. Jesus said:

> <u>John 6:37-40:</u> *"All that the Father gives Me shall come to Me, and the one who comes to Me <u>I will certainly not cast out</u>. For I have come down from heaven, not to do My own will, but the will of Him who sent Me. And this is the will of Him who sent Me, that of all that He has given Me I lose nothing, but raise it up on the last day. For this is the will of My Father, that <u>everyone who beholds the Son and believes in Him, may have eternal life; and I Myself will raise him up on the last day</u>."*

Those in Christ are no longer under the judgment of the Law because Jesus was the fulfillment of the Law:

> <u>Romans 8:1-4:</u> *"THERE is therefore now no condemnation for those who are in Christ Jesus. For the law of the Spirit of life in Christ Jesus has set you free from the law of sin and of death. For what the Law could not do, weak as it was through the flesh,*

God did: sending His own Son in the likeness of sinful flesh and as an offering for sin, He condemned sin in the flesh, in order that the requirement of the Law might be fulfilled in us, who do not walk according to the flesh, but according to the Spirit."

APPENDIX 2 of 2

A GENERAL OUTLINE OF FOUNDATIONAL DOCTRINES OF BIBLICAL CHRISTIANITY

True fundamental doctrines are derived from *Scripture alone* and do not originate from religious tradition or ecclesiastical groups or counsels. Oswald Chambers stated:

> "We are apt to forget that a man is not only committed to Jesus Christ for salvation; he is committed to Jesus Christ's view of God, of the world, of sin and of the devil, and this will mean that he must recognize the responsibility of being transformed by the renewing of his mind."[11]

A mature Christian is committed to the Bible to formulate his theological beliefs. From the study of Scripture, one will affirm the following doctrines:[12]

---

[11] Chambers, O. (1993, c1935). *My Utmost for His Highest: selections for the year* (September 9). Grand Rapids, MI: Discovery House Publishers.

[12] The outline is largely, but not exclusively from: MacArthur, J. (1994). *Reckless faith: When the church loses its will to discern.* p.102. Wheaton, Ill.: Crossway Books.

- **Inspiration, Inerrancy and Authority of Scripture:** Christ is the Word of God incarnate: John 1:1,14, 2 Peter 1:20-21, 2 Timothy 3:16, Proverbs 30:5-6, Revelation 22:18-19.

- **Virgin Birth:** Matthew 1:18-25, Luke 1:34-35, John 1:14.

- **The Deity of Jesus Christ, The Son of God:** He is God incarnate (God in a human flesh-and-blood body): Colossians 2:9, 1 John 5:20, Titus 2:13-14, John 8:58 and 10:30, Mark 14:61-62, John 20:28, Mark 15:39, John 21:14, Luke 22:70, John 20:31.

- **Jesus' Humanity:** His incarnation (1 John 4:2-3); He was tempted (Luke 4:1-13), hungry (Matthew 4:2), thirsty (John 19:28), slept (Matthew 8:24), died (Mark 15:39-45, Matthew 27:50).

- **Jesus' Sinlessness:** 2 Corinthians 5:21, Hebrews 4:15, 1 Peter 2:22, 1 John 3:5.

- **The Trinity:** Father, Son and Holy Spirit. There is one God who eternally exists in three persons. Each possesses the same nature and attributes but is distinct in office and activity: Deuteronomy 6:4, Matthew 28:19, John 10:30, John 17:21,

John 10:38, 1 John 2:20-24. Jesus is the Son of God and Savior (John 20:31).

- **Jesus—Worker of Miracles, All-Powerful and Creator of All Things:** John 11:32-45, Matthew 12:22, Luke 7:21-23, Matthew 15:30-31, Mark 9:23, 10:27, Luke 1:37, 18:27; Creator of All Things: John 1:3, John 1:10, 1 Corinthians 8:6, Revelation 4:11, Genesis 1:1, Colossians 1:15-17, Hebrews 1:2.

- **Human Depravity:** Each person is morally corrupt and sinful which is the condition of being spiritually dead toward God: Romans 3:23, Ephesians 2:1-3, Ecclesiastes 7:20, Romans 5:12, Psalms 14:1-3, Romans 3:20, Psalms 143:2, Psalm 51:5.

- **Christ's Atoning Death and Bodily Resurrection:** Christ died on the cross as a substitutionary sacrifice for sinners: 1 Peter 3:18, 2 Corinthians 5:21, 1 Corinthians 15:1-7, Titus 2:13-14, Romans 5:12-21, Hebrews 2:14, John 11:25-27, John 4:25-26, 1 John 2:1-2, John 21:14.

- **A Person is Saved from Eternal Damnation by God's Grace Through Faith in Jesus Christ and His Sacrificial Payment for Sin by His Death on The Cross (and nothing else):** One is not saved by works of righteousness, being a good person, or attempted obedience to the Law: Ephesians 2:8-10, Galatians 2:16 - 3:8, Romans 4:4-5, Romans 3:27-31, 5:11-21, Acts 10:43, Titus 2:13-14, John 3:15-18.

- **The Lordship of Christ:** Romans 10:9: *"...that if you confess with your mouth Jesus as Lord, and believe in your heart that God raised Him from the dead, you will be saved;"* John 13:13: *"You call Me Teacher and Lord; and you are right, for so I am."* See also Philippians 2:8-11, 1 Corinthians 16:22-23, Romans 14:9, Acts 16:31, 1 Corinthians 12:3, Acts 2:21 and 36, Acts 1:21, Matthew 12:8, Matthew 22:37, Isaiah 45:23, Romans 14:11.

- **The Return of Christ:** Second Coming: John 14:1-3, Matthew 26:64, Luke 12:40, Matthew 24:27 and 42-51, Mark 14:62, John 21:21-23, Mark 13:26.

- **The Eternal Damnation in Hell for the Unsaved:** John 15:6, Revelation 20:10-15, Revelation 21:8, John 3:18, 1 Corinthians 6:9-11, 2 Thessalonians 1:8-9, John 5:22, Mark 9:43-48.

- **Eternal Reign Of Christ in Heaven and Eternal Life for those He Redeemed:** John 14:1-3, Matthew 19:28-29, Matthew

25:46, John 3:15-16, Revelation 4:5-11,
1 John 5:20, Jude v.21, 1 Peter 4:11, 1 John
1:2-4, Titus 2:13-14.

---

* Fundamental doctrines are those that are essential to one making a claim to true Biblical Christianity. What are the fundamentals of the faith? Most restrict the list of fundamental doctrines to those that relate to the issue of salvation alone (soteriological—the theological doctrine of salvation in Christianity). "Historically, fundamentalism has been used to identify one holding to the five fundamentals of the faith adopted by the General Assembly of the Presbyterian Church in the U.S.A. in 1910. The five fundamentals were: the miracles of Christ, the virgin birth of Christ, the substitutionary atonement of Christ, the bodily resurrection of Christ, and the inspiration of Scripture. Fundamentalism has stood for the historic fundamentals of Christianity, particularly as developed in *The Fundamentals*. These were initially issued as twelve booklets edited by R. A. Torrey and A. C. Dixon." Enns, P. P. (1997, c1989). *The Moody Handbook of Theology* p. 613. Chicago, Ill.: Moody Press. The reason for limiting it to the doctrine of salvation is due to the awesome and wonderful simplicity of becoming a true Christian! Romans 10:9: *"...that if you confess with your mouth Jesus as Lord, and believe in your heart that God raised Him from the dead, you will be saved...."*

www.ingramcontent.com/pod-product-compliance
Lightning Source LLC
Chambersburg PA
CBHW070633150426
42811CB00050B/291